*a lo Cubano*

**The Cuban way.**

# HAVANA 101
## WAYS TO ROCK YOUR WORLD

### A BEGINNER'S GUIDE TO THE RHYTHM OF CUBA!

By DAYNA STEELE
and GRAHAM SOWA

Illustrated By **Carlos Paiffer**

**Daily Success**
THE BOOK SERIES

## OTHER BOOKS BY DAYNA STEELE

In the Classroom: 101 Ways to Rock Your World
with Linda Lee and Cheryl Evans

Welcome to College! 101 Ways to Rock
Your World
with Page Grossman

On the Golf Course: 101 Ways to Rock
Your World
with Aram Hudson and Cathy Arroyo

101 Ways to Rock Your World:
Everyday Activities for Success Every Day

Rock to the Top:
What I Learned about Success from the World's
Greatest Rock Stars

The tips in this book are merely suggestions based on the combined knowledge and experience of the authors.

## DEDICATED TO...

Mi Familia Justiz
*Dayna Steele*

Maylin and Gaby
*Graham Sowa*

# CONTENTS

*yuma*

**Foreigner (you).**

# INTRODUCTION

**A**fter 52 years of tourism restrictions, Cuba has unexpectedly emerged as the new frontier in U.S. travel. Any American who longs to visit this alluring, long-forbidden country will find *Havana: 101 Ways to Rock Your World* essential reading. Authors Dayna Steele and Graham Sowa have created more than a guidebook of places to see and things to do. *101 Ways…* is a friendly and conversational blueprint for how to set your expectations and prepare yourself for both the discoveries and idiosyncrasies of Cuban society.

Cuba has remained in our collective consciousness for more than a hundred years. Whether you identify the island with Havana's glamorous casinos of the 1950s, Fidel Castro and the Cuban Revolution, 1962's Missile Crisis, Roosevelt's Rough Riders, or the country's signature music, dancing, and cuisine, chances are that if you are a U.S. citizen, you have not yet seen Cuba up close.

For millions of Americans, our nation's embargo and ensuing travel restrictions against our near neighbor have created more than 50 years of curiosity and pent-up demand. Dayna and Graham's combined experience and obvious affection for Cuba make them the ideal guides to this fascinating country—and *Havana: 101 Ways to Rock Your World*, the perfect guidebook for any visitor to the island nation.

When I began traveling to Cuba, there was virtually no information about what to expect or how to navigate the country's unique complexities. The authors' personal approach makes learning *what every traveler needs to know* fun as well as informative. And there are *many* things the would-be traveler needs to know. One of the most important is flexibility: "going with the flow." Cubans call it "A lo Cubano:" Cuban-style. Essentially, it's the country's version of "Murphy's Law." Dayna and Graham explain this throughout *Havana: 101 Ways to Rock Your World*. The good news is, in Cuba, the spontaneous discovery often trumps the planned one. A couple of years ago, for instance, one of our tour groups set out for the city of Matanzas, about an hour and a half from Havana.

Once we arrived, we learned that the community project we were visiting was closed that day because of an obscure holiday. Never mind that we had confirmed the appointment one month, one week, and one day before. A few of the guests were upset, of course, that they had traveled all that way to have the activity cancelled. Others said, "Let's go with it, a lo Cubano." After some consideration, the guide suggested that the group of 16 visit his aunt, who lived about 20 minutes away. "We can see how Cubans live outside the city, up close and personal," the guide said. Once the group arrived, neighbors grew curious. After all, they hadn't met many Americans. Within only a few hours, the neighborhood extended the hand of Cuban hospitality and welcomed them with a pig roast, singing, poetry, and celebration. The group stayed for six hours and made lifelong friends. It was an experience none of them will forget. Asi es la vida en Cuba.

As president of insightCuba, I've sent Americans to Cuba legally since 2000. Some years ago, a guest told me, "Cuba only takes a minute to fall in love with, but will take a lifetime to understand." The insider knowledge in *Havana: 101 Ways to Rock Your World*, will help shorten that learning curve.

Tom Popper
President
InsightCuba.com

insightCUBA

## ABOUT TOM POPPER:

Tom became insightCuba's president in 2002 after visiting Cuba for the first time. Under his leadership, insightCuba became the largest provider of people-to-people travel to Cuba. Tom has been interviewed by hundreds of newspapers and travel magazines, and featured on CNN, MSNBC, ABC, NBC, and radio stations nationwide.

*First World*

**Merriam-Webster dictionary definition: the countries of the world that have many industries and relatively few poor people.**

## OPEN

No KFC, McDonalds, or Starbucks. Havana is probably the last capital city in the western hemisphere where, no matter how well-stocked you are with cash, technology, and First World confidence, you are going to have to get to know the city on its terms. In Havana, you will eat its food, listen to its music, and interact with its people. There has not yet been an all-out invasion of chain stores, fast food, and material culture from the United States...at least in the last 57 years.

We wrote these tips to help travelers, mostly fellow United States citizens, who will be visiting this Caribbean city by the millions in the next decade. Our goal is to help set reasonable expectations for your trip. The global cultural success of the United States has made traveling to many exotic places in the world relatively easy because when you show up things end up looking, and functioning, as they do back home. Not so much in Havana. The city can present mind-boggling, frustrating and nonsensical conundrums that are the blight, or pleasure, of getting to know a place very different from where you grew up. If you don't know what to expect, things are more difficult than they need to be.

For me, Cuba is the closest place to the United States where you can show up and feel like you are far, far away from home. Wireless connections are few and far between, data plans are unheard of, and roaming is not something your cell phone does, it is something you do. Havana is where I can wring myself out and try to be less self-absorbed. Interacting with the locals is key. If you are an introvert, don't worry, they will usually take the initiative. Discussing politics, family life, sports, art, religion, and everything under the sweltering Caribbean sun is fair game with most Cubans. It is what I enjoy most about sitting down and spending time with people from here. These are the moments when we most often stand on common ground with respect to our experiences, expectations, and desires – despite our cultural differences.

When I met Dayna Steele and her family in the sweltering Terminal 2 of Havana's Jose Martí

International Airport, we didn't have so much time for sunny self-reflection. There was lost luggage, a delayed flight, and surly customs agents... and nowhere to sit or buy water. I knew overcoming this first impression and finding the numerous redeeming qualities of Havana would be an uphill battle. Fortunately, Dayna was more than game at giving Havana a second, and even third chance. The rewards were great enough that we decided to write a book to help others set their expectations when they visit Havana.

Despite the old American cars and lack of infrastructure development, Cuba and its capital are dynamic places. Change seems to be coming more quickly with every passing day. You can once again get a *Havana Libre* cocktail made with Coca-Cola, and you won't be the only American on your flight or at your hotel. But still, don't expect to see more than a few token reminders of your lifestyle at home when you come. Be ready to get to know the city, and its residents, the Cuban way.

As quickly as Havana is changing, the United States policy towards Cuba is changing even quicker. Guidebook editors all over the world are realizing their most recent Cuba edition is out of date before it even goes to press. Keeping this rapid pace of change in mind, we tried to make these tips as specific to Havana and Cuba as possible but also general enough to have staying power for the next few years. Just as there are new ways to travel from the United States to Cuba every month, there is a new best restaurant in Havana every week. We are not going to pretend that we are able to keep up with all of this change and write a "definitive" guide. Instead, we hope you can use these travel tips as a solid foundation by which to begin to explore the city. This book, an easy-to-read map, and a willingness to take to the streets and explore will likely lead you to places in Havana that even the best travel guides haven't found.

Graham Sowa
Havana, Cuba resident
2010-2016

# BEFORE YOU GO

*Change is hard – in our own lives, and in the lives of nations. And change is even harder when we carry the heavy weight of history on our shoulders. But today we are making these changes because it is the right thing to do. Today, America chooses to cut loose the shackles of the past so as to reach for a better future – for the Cuban people, for the American people, for our entire hemisphere, and for the world.*

**President Barrack Obama**
**December 17, 2014**

# 1. DO YOUR HOMEWORK.

If you are used to ticking a few boxes, putting in your credit card information and booking travel, then Cuba will be an atypical experience. The best way to make the process more convenient is to be educated. The relationship between Cuba and the United States began to change on December 17, 2014. Since then, the changes have increased from monthly to weekly to daily. These modifications include rules governing if you can go, to how you can get there, to what you can do while you are there and what you can bring back with you when you leave. Your first move should be to check out what's new in the last few weeks. Going to Cuba is getting easier, and you should strive to make your trip easier as well. You are going to meet other tourists on the island. Why not make them a bit jealous with your Havana travel knowledge prowess? The U.S. Treasury Department routinely publishes new travel guidelines for American citizens and Internet travel forums are usually the most up to date spots to check out the opinions of other in-the-know tourists.

## 2. CHECK YOUR PASSPORT.

If your passport is going to expire within the next six months before you complete your travel, you can't travel to Cuba – and many other places. Your passport must have at least half a year left before the expiration date. Cuban authorities are professionals at bureaucracy, and while you can talk your way out of some problems, immigration law is not one of them. On the same note: don´t overstay your Cuban visa, which is still required at this writing. Renew it at least a week before it expires.

## 3. MAKE A BUDGET.

**H**avana is a cosmopolitan city with two econo-
mies: one for people who make miserly wag-
es in their government jobs and one for tourists
and other economically privileged people. While
it´s possible to do Havana on a budget, smart first-
time travelers should plan as if they are going to
a moderate First World city as far as spending
projections go. This spending applies to hotels,
meals, entertainment and more. Just like with any
vacation, avoid surprises by making a budget and
sticking to it.

**Notes:**

*Never go on trips with anyone you do not love.*

**Ernest "Papa" Hemingway, lover of Cuba**

## 4. INVITE A FRIEND.

**"I** wish I could go!" will be the most common response when you get back from your trip to Havana. Go ahead and preempt that by inviting a friend (or several) to share the trip with you. Havana has a reputation for being one of the safest destinations in Latin America and the Caribbean but traveling in numbers is always a good safety idea. Traveling in pairs or more makes things like booking a hotel, taking taxi-cabs, and joining excursions more economical. You can always split off and do your own thing once in Havana and re-group for sundowners and stories in the evenings.

## 5. SET REALISTIC EXPECTATIONS.

For many of us, the idea of a Caribbean vacation means being able to shut off the part of our brain controlling moderation and assume everything will be fun and easy. Havana is not so forgiving. The city is almost 500 years old, and it looks it in many places. Lights go off, even in nice hotels, and your water might not always be hot, or even running. Similarly, 57 years of communism hasn´t exactly created a service industry that makes the customer feel valued or even wanted. And, if you consider yourself punctual, you should prepare yourself for "island time."

# 6. DUST OFF YOUR DANCING SHOES.

**M**usic and dancing are the heart and soul of Cuba. Read, watch videos, get in front of a mirror, and learn at least a few basic steps so you can fake your way around the dance floor with a resemblance of grace. Just getting the simple stuff correct will be enough to impress fellow travelers and locals alike. All music genres in Cuba are celebrated, from salsa and rumba to punk and rock to bachata and more.

*chivo*

**If you buy cigars on the street, the seller will look over their shoulder to make sure no "chivos" are around, a snitch.**

## 7. PRACTICE SPANISH.

You may not be able to speak a word of Spanish. And yes, people may laugh at you in Cuba when you try. But they will appreciate the fact you have tried, and it will make you feel more like a local when you can spot a *chivo* or can let out a loud *PINGA!* when you stub your toe. Don't know what those words mean? Look through this book for the translations and many more useful phrases.

*pinga*

**Very vulgar explicative that is frequently used by adults and school children alike. Don´t be afraid to let this out when you just can´t take it anymore.**

## 8. LOOSEN UP.

The reason Cubans can tell you are a foreigner, besides the fact your shoes are probably a lot newer than theirs, is you are a bit stiff. Cubans have a swagger when they walk, a sway when they dance, and even their Spanish sounds so loose it´s about to fall apart. So, before you leave home - take a stretch, shake out the kinks, and loosen up. A lo Cubano.

*casa particular*

A privately owned home that rents out to foreigners. These bed and breakfast type establishments have been around for 20 years. Stay
with a Cuban family and get an even closer-
to-authentic Havana experience.

## 9. DOWNLOAD APPS.

As of May 2015, there are still no cell phone or mobile data plans for U.S. cell phone carriers in Havana. It's coming, but slowly. That means you have to dial back your brain to a pre-internet 24/7 mentality and do a bit of planning. If you just can´t bring yourself to go back to the dead-tree edition of books and using paper and pen, then you need to download apps that will work offline. A good Cuba app will have a detailed map of Havana and major cities, a listing of hotels, *casa particulares*, restaurants, and other service industries. Havana Good Time, Triposo Cuba, and Conoce Havana are good places to start.

## 10. INVEST IN TRAVEL INSURANCE.

As the relationship between Cuba and the United States changes, unexpected things will happen. Be prepared. Buy the offered travel insurance through your travel tour company or airline. It's like CPR – you hope you never need it, but boy, are you glad you have it when you do.

## 11. CHECK THE WEATHER.

**H**urricanes, cold fronts and tropical showers, oh my. Before getting to Havana, consider when you want to go. Summer months risk hurricanes, which, while very rare, could be disastrous. A winter visit can be overshadowed by cold fronts; not freezing, but rotten enough weather to keep you indoors. Check the weather for the time of year you want to visit Havana before you book your travel, then pack accordingly.

*¿Que bola?*

**What's up?**

## 12. CHECK EVENTS CALENDARS.

**H**avana´s cultural life is vibrant, but the lack of Internet as well as the overzealous use of phones for personal calls by theater and museum employees means finding out what is happening around town is a chore. The best bet is to check a cultural calendar at a website such as OnCuba. com or execute a simple Google search to see what is going on during your visit before you get there. If you have a penchant for ballet, jazz, Latin American movies, contemporary dance, art, marathons, or cigars, there are various festivals during the year you should consider attending. If you wait to see what´s going on when you arrive, you'll probably just end up at an oversold tourist trap.

*no es fácil*

It's not easy. What Cubans say when things don't go their way and there is nothing they can do to change the situation. Long line at immigration at the airport? No es fácil.

## 13. PACK LIGHT WITH SPACE TO SPARE.

**A**re we fleeing the apocalypse or going on vacation? Cubans traveling home or to visit their families on the island bring everything from a new set of truck wheels to 60" TVs. Lots of 60" TVs. The resulting check-in line is long, arduous, and patience testing. That is nothing compared to when you realize in the Jose Martí Airport in Havana that your bags were left behind so they could fit all the TVs on the plane. Avoid checking bags and roll with a carry-on. If you must check a bag, show up as early as possible to be sure yours might be one of the first on the plane. *No es fácil.* Also, leave space so you will have room for gifts, like the size and shape of cigar boxes, to take home.

*paladar*

Generic Cuban term for a privately owned restaurant. The first paladares opened in the mid-1990s but since the loosening of private business regulations, there have been more than 150 new restaurants and cafes opened in Havana since 2011. Come hungry.

## 14. WHAT CLOTHES TO PACK.

**D**ress code in Havana is very relaxed, but places such as the nice nightclubs or paladares still have requirements (a pair of slacks and decent shirt will do). If you plan beach or pool time bring a bathing suit (you won't find one to buy easily if you forget). A pair of good walking shoes is a must. And the cooler and more breezy your wardrobe, the better; high humidity is the norm in Havana.

## 15. REFILL PRESCRIPTIONS AND PACK OVER-THE-COUNTER MEDS.

**M**ost foreign travelers in Cuba pay for health insurance through their visa fee upon arrival in Havana or through the travel agent booking their travel. Coverage guarantees treatment and pays most of the associated costs at all island health centers including health tourism facilities such as Cira Garcia Clinic in Havana. That being said, don´t rely on Cuban health insurance to refill your meds. Even simple over-the-counter stuff such as Ibuprofen is distributed with a prescription in Cuba. Plan ahead and bring extras of everything you think you will need instead of losing time seeing a doctor and going to the international pharmacy. You can't always run to a store in Cuba and get what you need.

## 16. BRING HYGIENE PRODUCTS, SUNSCREEN, AND BUGSPRAY.

Just as it is with prescriptions and over-the-counter meds, you can't pop into a local drugstore and expect to grab hygiene products such as sunscreen or bug spray. And if you do find some, don't even think about brand selection. Shopping in Cuba is fun if you are browsing around looking for souvenirs or nothing in particular. If you are looking for something specific, it is mind-boggling. After going to two or three stores and not finding what you are looking for, go ahead and exclaim "*pinga!*" You can keep looking or admit defeat. Better yet, just pack it. *No es fácil.*

## 17. THINK ABOUT GIFTS.

Fifty-seven years of isolation has made acquiring material goods in Cuba difficult to impossible for many local families. While the situation is improving, there are still periodic shortages of basic food and hygiene items. Even when things are in stock, the selection is nothing like what the First World is used to. Bring a stash of small gifts to share with your new Cuban friends. A small bag of school supplies for your taxi driver, baseballs for neighborhood kids, a fancy bar of soap left with the tip for your room service at the hotel, or some of your favorite snacks for a guide at a museum will always make people smile and remember you. Cuba is still one of the few places in the world where you can give a person a stick of deodorant without them thinking you are suggesting they smell bad!

## 18. PACK SNACKS.

**B**ring something to munch on that reminds you of home – to eat and to share. Cuban street food includes doughy pizza, fried flour (*fritura de harina*), fried corn (*fritura de maiz*), and *croquetas* (a mix of flour, lard, and a bit of fish, fried of course). So unless you plan on carb-loading and you have a gastrointestinal tract impervious to hearty doses of grease, plan on bringing something healthy to munch on. Depending on the time of year, you may find fresh fruit for sale in the farmers markets located all through Havana. Bananas, mangoes, avocados, guava, and other fruits are available, depending on the season. Just be sure to wash any of these before indulging.

*Why pay $100 on a therapy session when you can spend $25 on a **cigar**?*

**Raul Julia**

## 19. BUY A HUMIDOR.

If you plan to bring back cigars from Cuba, you are going to need a humidor in order to store them properly. If you purchase one before you go, it will be ready to house those Cuban cigars when you return and keep them fresh. If you wait to buy one in Cuba, humidors can be bought at the official state-run Habanos Cigar stores. The same quality, and better selection, can be found at artisan markets like the Almacenes de San Jose on the Old Havana waterfront. Better yet, buying from artisans directly means you pay a fraction of the official store price. Whatever you decide to do, you need a humidor if you are going to purchase cigars to smoke at a later date. There is nothing so sad as a Cuban cigar gone bad.

*Murphy's Law*

**Anything that can go wrong, will go wrong.**

## 20. BRING UNIVERSAL ELECTRIC OUTLET ADAPTERS.

**E**ven at the best hotels in town, you might find a mix of different types of electrical outlets. Murphy´s Law applies to travelers here more than anywhere else in the world so none of these will match with your chargers or hair dryer. Save yourself the trip downstairs to the concierge, or worse, to the non-existent store to look for an adapter. Bring a good universal electric outlet adapter. Even better, bring two.

## 21. CHARGE YOURSELF AND YOUR BATTERIES.

**A**rrive in Havana all charged up and ready to go. You are now in the cosmopolitan third world where people move around constantly, the tropical heat can be oppressive, and having one more mojito always sounds like a good idea. Come here ready to hit the ground running and get a feel for the city. Don´t waste a second while you are here. If you need a recovery day, wait until you get home. Also, charge all of your personal electronics (cameras, nearly useless cell phones, etc.) both before arriving and going out each day. Finding a place to charge is difficult if not impossible, even in hotel lobbies or the airport.

## 22. DOUBLE AND TRIPLE-CHECK YOUR RESERVATIONS.

Cuba´s travel infrastructure supports millions of tourists each year but behind the scenes it mostly operates in the pre-digital age. Your reservation could be lost when a less-than-enthusiastic, underpaid hotel employee writes your name down on a scrap piece of paper (because their computer is out of service) and then someone else uses it as a napkin. When you arrive at the check-in desk there will be no record of your reservation, and you will be lucky to get a *no es fàcil* from the receptionist. Nip this potential problem in the bud; send emails and make phone calls confirming your reservations when you make them and again before you leave. Arrive in Havana with printed copies of all of those email confirmations.

## 23. BRING PLENTY OF CASH WITH YOU.

**E**ven with the recent changes, very few Havana establishments accept credit cards - nor will they for a while to come. Trying to get cash is a pain and will probably cost you at least a day of your vacation, not to mention all of your patience. Make sure you arrive with plenty of cash to cover all of your expenses in Cuba. Once you get settled in the country, find a safe place to store that cash, so you are not carrying it all around with you and risk losing it. Hotel safes and money belts are good things to have and use in Havana.

## 24. SET YOUR ALARM CLOCK.

**M**ost flights to Havana leave early, and the check-in lines can be brutal (remember the 60" TVs?). On top of it all, the check-in time for charter flights is 4 hours before the flight leaves, which means you have to be stepping into the airport terminal around 4:00 AM. Do yourself and your travel companions a favor - set an alarm, get to bed early the night before, and be ready to go. You don't want to forget any last-minute items. Hopefully, once regularly scheduled commercial flights begin between Havana and cities in the United States, check-in times will be slightly saner. However, don't bet on the line of Cubans with TVs disappearing anytime soon.

# WHEN YOU ARRIVE

*permiso*

**Excuse me, pardon me. Repeated over and over in the hordes of Cubans and tourists everywhere you go.**

## 25. SAY *PERMISO*.

Once you arrive at the Havana airport, add the word *permiso* to your Cuban Spanish repertoire. You are probably going to encounter throngs of people, and there isn't a VIP lane. Cubans do things collectively (such as standing in horde-like lines) due to bread lines, bus lines, ice cream lines, etc. Their concept of personal space is limited to the molecules separating your shoulder from theirs. When you see your suitcase, go ahead, and plunge forward while saying *permiso*. Now it's time for the customs insanity. That´s right, *permiso*. Then there's leaving the airport and getting a cab...*permiso, permiso, permiso*. Remember, you can avoid one or two of these *permisos* if you packed light and didn't check luggage.

*cerveza*

**Beer.**

## 26. BREATH, LOOK, FEEL.

The airport might be a bit traumatizing, but don't be stressed out. There's a welcome party happening just outside the airport. Really. Even if it's nine in the morning, people are passing around a rum bottle while they wait for family to arrive from Miami. Get your first Cuban espresso or cerveza at the snack bar outside and breathe in the Caribbean air (yes, the smell of diesel goes away once you get closer to the ocean), look at all those old American cars (and their Russian and French counterparts), and feel the warm tropical sun. You are in Havana!

*cadeca*

**An official, safe place to change your money.**

## 27. CHANGE AND INSPECT YOUR MONEY.

Change a small amount of money at the airport when you arrive. In Havana, all of the official money changing offices are called "Cadecas." The rates are the same at all Cadecas and the only other place where you should change money is at the hotel reception desk (where the rate might be worse). No matter who offers what, don´t change anywhere but the Cadeca or your hotel. Once you get your Cuban cash, inspect it to make sure you were given the correct amount and that your receipt is also correct. Here's where it gets confusing. There is a two-currency system - Cuban Pesos and Convertible Pesos. Your foreign currency is always changed to Convertible Pesos, never Cuban Pesos, at least for now. The Cuban Government has pledged to eliminate the Convertible Peso sometime in 2016, leaving everyone with the Cuban Peso. Until then you should check to make sure you were not given the much less valuable Cuban Peso when you change money. To help tell the two apart the valuable Convertible Pesos are brighter colors and have images of monuments instead of people (the Cuban Pesos have images of people, like U.S. Currency). Remember that when you change U.S. dollars to Convertible Pesos, there is a 10% tax for U.S. dollars.

# Notes:

*menudo*

**Small change for tipping, coins, or a one-peso
bill.**

## 28. GET SMALL CHANGE.

Lackadaisical bathroom attendants, musicians, and street artists are all working for the coins in your pocket. You can ask for coins when you change money, but paying for small transactions with larger bills is the best way to keep your pockets jingling. Make it part of your morning routine to visit the hotel reception desk and trade in a few bills for coins; tell them it is for tipping and they should happily oblige your request. If you do get caught with an urge to use the restroom but don't have any *menudo*, don't fret, just walk in. When you gotta go, you gotta go.

## 29. STOP TRYING TO CHECK YOUR PHONE.

**S**orry, no matter how many times you look at your phone, you will not have gotten a message, email, tweet or any other form of wireless communication since arriving in Havana. Nor are you likely to get such a message, at least until Cubacel (the only, and state-owned, cell company) and the United States wireless providers come to a roaming agreement. Could be tomorrow, could be in 5 years. Until then, realize your phone is a very sophisticated camera and map ... as long as you remembered to download those offline Cuba apps. Once you get to your hotel, you will probably have some sort of expensive Wi-Fi service (make sure that's in your budget.) You can then communicate with someone back home using services such as Twitter or Facebook that seem to work everywhere. Skype and What's App work for some, not for others.

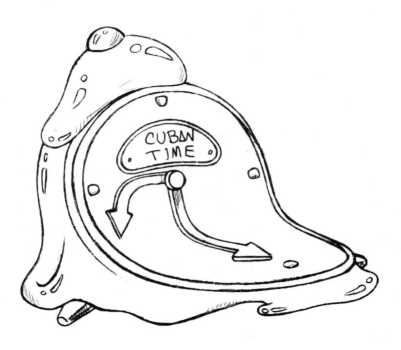

## 30. RESET YOUR INTERNAL CLOCK TO ISLAND TIME.

Since you set your expectations before getting to Havana, please reset your fast-paced, get-it-done-now attitude to somewhere between island slow and a sloth's metabolic rate. If something doesn't work out (*pinga!*) or if you find yourself waiting longer than expected (*no es fácil*), remember you are in Havana to explore the city on its terms. And on Havana's terms, things like departure and arrival times and store hours are more of suggestions than business policies. It might also help to know there are no open container laws and alcohol is sold 24/7 just about everywhere, plus there is rum called *Planchao* sold in a juice box, recently made famous by U.S. comedian Conan O'Brien. Get a *Planchao* and do it *a lo Cubano*. And, if you don't imbibe, make sure the juice box you (or your kids) are drinking is non-alcoholic juice.

*Havana: the gateway to the Gulf of Mexico.*

**Cuban Tourism Board**

## 31. DON'T BE AFRAID TO ASK FOR HELP.

If you find yourself lost, confused, or just want to know more about something you are looking at, don´t be shy to approach a stranger and ask. It is always better if you approach locals as opposed to locals coming to you. The latter are usually hustlers with ulterior motives that don't include being altruistic to a foreigner (i.e. money, gifts, commission for leading you to a *paladar* or *casa particular* etc.) Avoid these opportunists by taking the initiative and approaching a local. The vast majority of the people will try their best to help or show you someone who can.

## 32. PUT ON SUNSCREEN
## AND BUG REPELLANT.

It is never too soon to put on sunscreen. As good as Caribbean sun feels, those UV rays are tearing up your skin. No matter how much melanin your epithelium is rocking, slather on sunscreen before hitting the streets or the beach. Do the same with bug repellant. Mosquito-transmitted viral infections could ruin your vacation or worse. The best method of prevention is to cover your skin with clothing and mosquito repellant. Both species of mosquito spreading these diseases (dengue fever and chikungunya) are on the prowl primarily during daylight hours in Cuba so apply both as part of your morning routine.

## 33. DRESS THE PART.

Maybe you are coming to Havana from Buffalo, New York in January, and it's difficult to imagine walking around all day in board shorts and an open shirt with a tropical flower print motif. Bring these things; it's okay. Havana loves tourists. Don´t be afraid to show you are one. If you don´t own the stereotypical guayabera shirt, get one. Put on a straw fedora and walk around with your camera around your shoulder. It's fun, and comfortable, to play the part of the visitor to this kaleidoscope city.

## 34. HAVE A PLAN BUT BE FLEXIBLE.

While it is possible just to show up in Havana and do your trip on-the-fly, don't expect a stress-free experience. As independent travel is still in its nascent phases, it is advisable to show up with, at a minimum, hotel or casa-particular reservations, in-country transportation arrangements, and any special excursions requiring a guide. If you are a foodie, you are going to want to make your paladar reservations at least a week or two in advance (don't forget to reconfirm!). Save yourself the feeling of despair and have backup plans for when things don't go as you anticipated. Keeping your plans a bit vague, such as "see live jazz" will allow you to structure your schedule and will give you the flexibility to plan once you see your options. Remember, much of Cuba is not Internet-connected, so when you arrive, you will find stuff going on you didn't encounter in your research. Use a pencil (and eraser) and build flexibility into your agenda.

## 35. LEAVE GAPS IN YOUR SCHEDULE.

**D**oing more than three or four things a day in Havana is being an ambitious traveler. While the city is compact, and most of the tourist-world can be found in the Central Havana, Old Havana, Vedado, and Playa Miramar neighborhoods, don't expect to move around with First World quickness. Opening late, closing early, taking long lunch breaks and attending to family necessity often interrupts the Cuban work day. It's best to allow yourself a chunk of time (30 minutes to an hour) between everything you plan to do. You won't be stressed out when it is 4:00 P.M and you realize all you have done is eaten breakfast, visited an art gallery, and had a long, possibly boozy, lunch.

## 36. OFFER TO SHARE A CAB.

If you are traveling independently, save yourself money and perhaps meet new travel companions by sharing a cab from the airport. Most hotels in Havana are clumped together on the south side of town so if you are a bit of an extrovert, it shouldn't be too much of a problem finding someone to share a ride. Usually, anyone seated on top of his or her luggage outside the airport thumbing through a travel guidebook is a likely candidate.

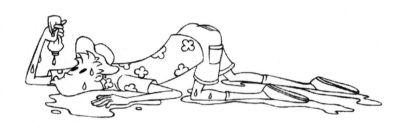

## 37. HYDRATE.

High humidity and tropical heat means you are going to sweat ... a lot. Stay ahead of the hydration game and start drinking water as soon as you arrive. Though the water is safe to drink in most parts of Cuba, sticking to bottled water is a good bet. Buy a couple of 1.5-liter bottles to take with you to your hotel room and some smaller bottles for walking around Havana. At restaurants, water is not always served unless asked for so as tempting as cold beer is, remember to start with something non-alcoholic. Hydrating with water goes for nighttime activities as well. Alternating between alcohol-based drinks and water is more likely to mean you will be functional the next day.

*'tabien*

The shorten version of esta bien as in "it's okay" or "okay". Cubans frequently use contractions so don't feel bad if your high school Spanish classes are not holding up as you expected.

## 38. HAVE A LAUGH!

**P**roblems? Inconvenience? If you need inspiration for how to handle problems in Cuba, just look to the Cubans themselves. Watch a bus stop for long enough and you will see it first-hand. Eventually, a bus will just pass by the stop and make everyone run another block to catch up … and most will be laughing. Yes, where you come from people would be on their phones tweeting this to the City Commissioner but in Havana, people redress their grievances with laughter. Maybe it's not fair, and it won't set things right, but it is a good way to keep the culture shock from getting under your skin and messing with your vacation.

## 39. PUT ON YOUR COMFORTABLE SHOES.

**E**ven if you dress to the nines when traveling, keep a pair of sneakers or good sandals handy to change into once in Havana. You will be walking a lot, and standing much more than you do at home. Save your feet and prevent creeping lower-back pain halfway into your visit by changing into comfortable, usable footwear from the get-go.

*candela* or *en llama*

**Literally both mean "on fire" but colloquially these synonyms are used as an exclamation of a problem. Use one of these when the hotel receptionist tells you your room isn't ready.**

## 40. BE AN ACTIVE PROBLEM SOLVER.

When your air conditioner won't turn on in your hotel room, don't think a call to the front desk will take care of the problem. Most likely your problem will be added to an infinite list that may or may not be addressed long after you check out. Go downstairs and talk to the reception desk, be polite, find out who the maintenance person is and offer to show him or her to your room. This type of handholding is the best way to be an active problem-solver in Cuba and get a positive outcome. Patience is key, but don't let patience become complacency. Show that you want to help out and be proactive which in turn will motivate everyone else. Don't forget to leave helpful individuals with a gratuity - a small tip or gift will do.

## 41. ORGANIZE YOUR TRAVEL DOCUMENTS.

Traveling to Cuba means abandoning the convenience of paperless electronic travel. Do you know, or remember, how to keep track of all of those travel documents? After taking out your passport, visa, plane ticket, and immigration forms half a dozen times, they will probably be scattered around your pockets, backpack, and suitcase. When you are finished with the airport routine, take a few minutes to organize yourself and make sure you haven't left anything. Making a trip back to the airport to try to find something will take up a half a day at best. If you are traveling with kids, or adults who might as well be kids, this goes double for you.

## 42. CHECK IN WITH SOMEONE BACK HOME.

Once you get your baggage, clear customs, run the airport gauntlet and get outside, your sensory overload combined with lack of cell phone signal will probably leave you forgetting you left loved ones back home who are wondering if you made it or not. Not to worry; many hotels have Wi-Fi. Buy a very short piece of Internet time and let someone know you have arrived safely. Make sure they have a phone number and room number of where you are staying if they need to get in touch. Then log off, look up, and enjoy Havana.

# IN HAVANA

*guayabera*

**A style of shirt worn by many Cubans.**

## 43. COMFORT WINS OVER STYLE.

**B**eing in Havana means being comfortable. Don't try to compare yourself to the locals who go out dressed to the nines. They have a lifetime of practice walking in those stilettoes, and their pores are trained not to sweat even under a swanky jacket. Keep your clothing options cool, breezy, and comfortable.

## 44. FIND SHADE.

**H**avana can be a sunny place. Combine that with sunlight reflected off of marble facades and plenty of humidity, vision, as well as comfort, becomes a challenge. Keep an eye out for the best place to stand without having to wipe your brow four times a minute. Don´t be the tourist squinting at a guidebook in the middle of the historic square; look around and find the shade.

*Twenty years from now you will be more disappointed by the things you didn't do than by the ones you did do.*

**Mark Twain**

## 45. BE AN IMPULSE BUYER.

**"M**aybe I will come back for it later," is not a reasonable phrase in Havana. Later will probably be never and, if you do get the chance to come back, whatever it was you decided you can't live without is gone. Stores seem to be stocked randomly, and basic items are always missing. If you see it and need it, buy it. Shopping for souvenirs and gifts should be done the same way. Except for the nearly ubiquitous cigars, rum and coffee (which can be bought easily enough at the Duty-Free on your way out) make your purchases as you go along. Trying to make return trips to specific places will probably leave you scurrying around, with no luck, on your last day in Havana.

*no gracias*

**No thank you.**

## 46. SAY *NO GRACIAS*.

In Havana, lots of people will approach you unsolicited. "Where are you from?" they might ask in near-perfect English. Amazingly, no matter how obscure your hometown is, they almost always have a cousin or close relative living there! Funny how that works out. The story will end with needing to buy milk for a baby, shoes for a kid in school or another heartbreaking necessity. Tread with care when people approach you, and you are not the initiator of the conversations. Sure - ask for help, talk to locals - but don´t get taken for a ride. Anytime someone talks to you, and you don´t feel like entertaining him or her, a firm "*no gracias*" will send them on their way. No matter what you wear or how you try to blend in, people will offer to sell you cigars, CDs, to play live music – you name it. If you don´t want it, say "*no gracias*" and move along.

## 47. TIP.

**G**oing out to listen to live music and all the tables are reserved? Five to ten dollars will magically make one appear. No more tickets to see Swan Lake? Want the same cab driver to pick you up after your night out? Make it worth their while. Good service? Go ahead and leave a tip. Just like in the United States, most wait staff in Cuba are paid very little money (usually a daily wage, not even hourly) and survive off of tips. If you go to *paladares*, you will probably have a decent meal and a waiter who knows what they are doing. Go ahead and leave an extra 10-15% for them on top of your bill. But beware; many places have begun including a "service charge" that will be listed on your bill. If that is the case, then the tip is already included.

## 48. STEP WITH CARE.

**M**any parts of Havana have sparse or no lighting at night, combined with uncovered manholes and broken sidewalks this can make a treacherous walk back to your hotel or casa particular. Be careful where you step and be smart about the path you choose to take home. Don´t feel envious when you see Cuban women navigating cobblestone streets in high heels, they have had lots of practice.

## 49. GET UP EARLY –
## AT LEAST ONE DAY.

**W**aking up early in Havana is the best way to see the structure of the city. Take a stroll outside as the sun is rising and see the light hit the buildings in Vedado or the long shadows cast over narrow streets in Havana Vieja. At this time of day, the streets are empty, so you have time to concentrate and look up. Check out the architecture and the tranquility. And, in what other cosmopolitan city can you hear so many roosters crow to announce the arrival of a new day?

## 50. TRY A RUM THAT ISN'T CALLED HAVANA CLUB OR A CIGAR THAT ISN'T COHIBA.

These two brands get all the press and worldwide fame but for what Cuba lacks in selection of other products, it more than makes up for in rum and cigars. Santero, Cubay, Santiago, and Mulata offer a wide range of aged rums. Montecristo, Romeo y Julieta, and H. Upmann offer premium cigars that smoke distinctly from the ubiquitously promoted Cohiba. This is a good time to stop being a tourist and enjoy what the locals know is good!

## 51. WALK ON THE MALECÓN

The Malecón is Havana´s seawall, and it stretches the length of three city neighborhoods: Vedado, Central Havana and Havana Vieja. On calm summer nights, it is a party stretching the length of the city. During the day, it is soaked in sun and a favorite spot to take colorful pictures of the dilapidated buildings that make up the façade of the city. Take a walk along this famous stretch of pavement, but look out for slippery patches of concrete. If the weather is stormy, the waves put on a show that rivals the fountains of hotels in Las Vegas as they crash into the concrete barrier.

*hablar mierda*

**Talking shit. It's what you do with good friends, fine Cuban rum, and a Cuban cigar.**

## 52. ENJOY THE HOTEL NACIONAL PATIO OVERLOOKING THE MALECÓN.

The Hotel Nacional de Cuba is an excellent location to look out over the Malecón while enjoying a fine Cuban cigar and premium Cuban rum. Clocking in at almost 90 years old, the hotel boasts shady gardens and your own personal perch overlooking the Atlantic Ocean. Close your eyes and imagine those who have come before you and enjoyed these same magnificent Cuban pleasures over the decades. Be careful. You could get used to this life quickly.

## 53. BRING AN UMBRELLA.

The tropics are notorious for getting you wet with your sweat and then dumping rain on you during the afternoon. Solve both problems with an umbrella. It will help keep the sun off during the day and will save you from a soaking when a sudden shower tries to ruin your stroll in Old Havana. If you forgot yours and it starts raining, just look around. An enterprising Cuban just might run out of a store or house with several umbrellas to sell at a premium.

## 54. NEGOTIATE FIRST AND CARRY EXACT CHANGE.

Taxis, club covers, bottle service, art, souvenirs, pretty much anything without a price tag - go ahead and settle on a clear price before committing yourself. Most service providers in Cuba are professionals and won´t try to take your wallet for a ride, but some will. Setting a clear price and even better, carrying exact change, avoids them upping the price or using the "sorry, I don´t have change" routine to cheat you out of a few dollars. Most hotel desks are happy to make change for you, so change a few big bills into smaller ones before you head out for the day or night. Or when you are out sightseeing, pay for a bottle of water with a larger bill and keep the change handy.

## 55. RIDE IN A CONVERTIBLE.

**P**ut on your best Caribbean tourist outfit and catch a ride in a convertible. Every car has a story, and every driver is a character. There is something about driving one of the iron blasts from the past that makes the chauffeurs want to impress foreigners with tall tales and witty comments. The joy of riding around Havana in style mixed with a frank conversation with a resident of the city is one of the best ways to get orientated geographically and culturally. Go convertible shopping; find the make, model, and color you want, negotiate a price and enjoy the ride.

## 56. GO TO THE BEACH.

A 15-minute cab ride east of Havana takes you to the aptly named Playas del Este (the eastern beaches) where Havana goes to soak up the sun and cool off in the Atlantic Ocean. It is close enough to make it back for your dinner reservations at a swanky paladar but far enough away to escape from the trappings of city life. Besides, don't miss out on the opportunity to hang out with Havana's population at their favorite summertime getaway. Just don't leave your belongings unguarded on the sand; they have a habit of walking away. Some beaches have facilities where someone will get you a chair and an umbrella and watch your stuff for a few pesos. Even then, it is still not a good idea to bring much of value. Leave that in the hotel safe.

## 57. GESTICULATE LIKE YOU MEAN IT.

**D**on´t be shy to wave your arms a bit, pucker your lips, or furrow your brow and nose. As if Cubans don´t converse at a loud enough volume, they also add a variety of gestures to their discourse. Learn how to point with your lips, cross your arms after you finish making a point or scrunch up your face when you don´t understand something. These actions will get you all kinds of street cred with the locals.

## 58. ASK FOR DIRECTIONS.

Lucky for the traveler Havana is a city of Spanish colonial design, which means streets run perpendicular and parallel, mostly in the cardinal directions. However, the one-way roads and lots of pedestrian traffic can challenge even the best internal compass. Don't be afraid to stick your head out your window (if you are driving) and ask how to get to where you are going. If you are on foot, you can stop almost anyone and ask for orientation. Just be careful about asking for help reading a map - that may confuse the situation more (Cubans use landmarks more than street names). Also, many streets have a pre- and post-revolutionary name so what it says on your map and what someone tells you can vary. Middle-aged and elderly people are the best to ask because they are less likely to give you the run-around or bug you for money after helping out.

*jiniteros*

**Street hustlers.**

# 59. IGNORE THE HUSTLERS.

Hustlers, locally known as *jiniteros*, will do their best to get you into a restaurant, casa particular, taxi, show, sell you cigars, sex and pretty much anything else they think a vacationer in Havana might want. If you are not interested, simply ignoring their advances is often enough to get them to focus their attention elsewhere. If you are walking alone, especially in touristy areas such as Old Havana, Central Havana, or the Malecón, putting in your ear buds and listening to music makes even the most aggressive *jinitero* abandon his mission. If they are insistent, just remember *"no gracias"*. When you use hustlers to take you around, expect to hear all kinds of sob stories as they look for tips. Plus, you will pay higher prices as business owners give a commission to *jiniteros* for bringing customers through the doors.

## 60. STAY AT A CASA PARTICULAR.

A *casa particular* is best defined as a Cuban bed and breakfast. Havana offers everything from ocean view penthouses for over $1,000 USD a night to dives with a sketchy mattress in the bad part of town for $5 USD. Be sure the *casa* you are staying in has a license (you will see a blue sticker that looks like a house on or near the front door). Don't be afraid to shop around and find a house, and owner, you like. Often the owners know what is going on in Havana and can arrange reliable transportation and recommend good restaurants. If you want to book a *casa particular* online, be sure it has strong and reputable reviews or you are booking through a trusted website such as airbnb. com. *Casa* stays are still one of the best ways to get to know Havana through the people who live and work there.

*comida criolla*

**Rice, beans, and the 3 "P"s - puerco, pescado, and pollo (pork, fish and chicken).**

## 61. EAT AT ONLY ONE STATE-OWNED RESTAURANT AND VARIOUS PALADARES.

**H**avana used to have a reputation for not having many restaurants worth eating at. That changed when rules governing private restaurants loosened in 2011. *Paladares* (Cuban for private restaurant) are now all the rage and have reopened the possibility for foodies to explore Havana via knife and fork. Even with the *paladar* explosion, there are still plenty of state-owned restaurants. Try one out for lunch or dinner and you can compare what the food scene used to be in Havana. Then spend the rest of your time dining at privately owned restaurants.

## 62. ASK SOMEONE WHAT HIS OR HER OTHER JOB IS.

**D**ue to low-paying state jobs and high-paying tourist jobs, Havana is full of doormen who have doctorates in engineering, taxi drivers who are also emergency room physicians, and waiters who could explain the more complicated aspects of quantum physics. Strike up a conversation with a hotel, restaurant, or transportation worker and ask them what their other job is. You might be surprised to find the person unloading your luggage at the hotel could also be designing Havana's next skyscraper (if any were being built).

*D17*

What locals call December 17, 2014 - one of the most significant dates in U.S.-Cuban history marking the beginning of improved relations between the two countries.

## 63. SEND A POSTCARD.

Getting a postcard in the days of social media and instant communications is quaint. Getting a postcard from Havana is mind-blowing. Surprise someone who didn't know you were going on the trip, or one of those friends who said it was impossible to travel to Cuba. Fair warning, it might take a few weeks (or months) for it to get delivered (if at all) so it may not be the best way to send birthday greetings! Ask for stamps and mail service in hotel lobbies or at a post office.

## 64. KEEP YOUR VALUABLES SAFE ...

**●●● I**n a safe. Hotels and many *casa particulares* offer safes to keep valuables, cash and travel documents. Use the safe. Going to Havana means having to carry around lots of cash since credit cards are not accepted in many places (yet), and international banking almost doesn't exist. Also, if you are from the United States of America, it's not a good idea to lose your passport. The U.S. Embassy will issue you a new one, but standing in line for a few hours will give you plenty of time to contemplate why you didn't store your documents in a place that was a little more secure.

## 65. SIT IN A PARK IN VEDADO.

Vedado is one of Havana's first master-planned residential communities. In between Central Havana and Playa, its tranquil streets and mansions (some crumbling, others restored) are separated by some of the city's best parks (some a bit overgrown, others meticulously maintained). Century-old trees shade wooden benches where you can sit and people-watch as Havana's residents live their lives. Escape the heat of the day and the hustle and bustle of the city by taking in some of Havana's green space… just like the Cubans do.

# Cuban Domino notes:

- *Four players make up two teams, team members play across from each other*
- *Shuffled, facedown, then each player draws 10 tiles that only they can look at. Any remaining dominoes are set aside and not used in further play.*
- *Players lay tiles. in turn counter-clockwise, onto the open ends of the domino layout with same-number adjacent to same-number (doubles placed horizontally onto ends, allowing play to branch four ways, and known as a spinner).*
- *Once a player has dominoed by setting their last tile, or the game is blocked with no player able to set a tile, the round is over and the player who dominoed or has the lowest total of pips left in their hand is the winner of that round.*
- *The winner of a round then scores the total number of pips on all the other players' dominoes, minus the total number of pips on any remaining dominoes in their hand.*
- *Rounds are usually played until a player with 100 points wins the game.*
- *A winning team member starts the next round.*

## 66. PLAY OR WATCH A GAME OF DOMINOES.

**Y**ou will hear a domino game before you see it. Loud men accompanied by the sound of tiles being slammed down on a wooden table are tale-tell signs a heated match is not far off. Don´t be afraid to approach a game in progress, just don´t interrupt until the play is done. If you are brave and want to attempt to play the game, ask "*ultimo*" and stake out a position in line. Just don´t bet any money you aren´t willing to lose.

## 67. TOUR A CIGAR FACTORY DURING READING TIME.

Cigar factories are one of the few places in Havana where you can show up and see everyone furiously working away at their task. Rows of cigar rollers are seated in grand halls where the open windows allow the breeze to waft around the aroma of aged tobacco. To keep everyone entertained, there is a "reader" who orates the daily news in the morning and then reads from a novel in the afternoon. The younger generation of cigar rollers is more entertained by their headphones connected to their smartphone. Still, this is a tradition only enjoyed and seen in Havana.

## 68. FERRY AND WALK TO GIANT JESUS.

**N**o capital of a former Spanish colony would be complete without a giant Jesus with outstretched arms looking over the city from on high. To see Havana's rendition of this monument, grab the local ferry from Old Havana to Casa Blanca and walk up the few hundred steps. The bonus of this little excursion is a fantastic view of the city from this strategic piece of high ground. It is perfect for a late afternoon adventure to take in the sunset backlighting the Havana skyline.

*My grandmother would shanghai pilots at the Havana airport so they'd bring me cartons of mango baby food -- the only kind I'd eat. I learned to eat peach later. And in every carton, she'd slip in a Cuban record.*

**Gloria Estefan**

# 69. LISTEN TO LIVE MUSIC DAILY.

**H**avana compares to Austin, Texas, or New Orleans, Louisiana when it comes to providing opportunities to listen to a variety of live music for free or on the cheap every day of the week. Walking around tourist areas will expose you to the traditional Son Salsa beats and internationally recognizable Cuban tunes. But if you follow your eardrums off the beaten path Havana hosts a variety of jazz venues, merengue shows, and boleros and their ballads. Metal heads can blow their eardrums at Maxim Rock, Havana's dedicated rock venue. Rap and hip-hop happens everywhere from Central Havana to the eastern Havana neighborhood of Alamar. Young people flock to the *Fabrica de Arte* or The Corner to hear covers of the latest pop songs from the USA and Europe. The Yellow Submarine hosts nightly cover bands of the best classic rock (not always sung in the best English). Even if you just sit outside under the stars on the Malecón with a bottle of rum, you'll hear music – just be sure to tip the roving street musicians who stop to entertain you.

# 70. GET OFF THE TOURIST MAP.

**P**opular guidebooks often come with maps of the most visited areas of Havana. However, there are other neighborhoods that have hundreds of years of history and represent the reality of the present day city. Municipalities such as Cerro, La Lisa, and Boyeros are examples of parts of Havana where thousands of people live but hardly anyone visits. Surprise your convertible driver and tell them you want to go to one of those places as you cruise the streets of Havana. They will probably be impressed by your local knowledge and willingness to get off the beaten path.

## 71. THINK TWICE ABOUT
## THE TROPICANA.

The infamous Tropicana nightclub is nowhere close to the action (far out in the boonies of Miramar). If you do go, you have been warned: once you decide you want to move on to something better for the night, the long taxi ride will probably put you to sleep. Don't risk it! The Tropicana nightclub is historic, raved about, and romantic: yes. Old, overpriced, a long drive and under-produced: some say yes. Save your money and time – unless you have lots of both.

**Notes:**

## 72. EXPLORE TRANSPORTATION OPTIONS.

Convertibles and old cars are all over Havana, but those are not the only ways to get around. Horse-drawn carriages, tricycle taxis, coco taxis (a motorized trike shaped like a coconut), motorcycles with sidecars, and ferries make up the varied forms of transportation in the city. You can even rent bicycles from places such as Taller Velo in Havana's Vedado neighborhood and explore the city with pedal power. Depending on where you are and how far you are going, don't be shy to experiment with different forms of getting around.

# BEFORE YOU DEPART

*gracias*

**Thank you.**

## 73. SAY *GRACIAS.*

**W**as someone super-helpful during your trip? Maybe it was the hotel concierge who got you last-minute concert tickets, or a cab driver who shuttled you home in the wee hours of the morning, or the receptionist who was able to get you checked in without having to wait for the bus loads of tour groups ahead of you. If someone went out of their way, try your best to reach out and tell them thanks. The tourist industry in Havana is about money just like anywhere else, but that is no reason you can´t put a human element into it now and then. That kindness is much appreciated in Cuba. And everywhere.

## 74. PICK UP GIFTS FOR
## THE FOLKS BACK HOME.

Coffee, rum, and cigars are the most-expected gifts by your friends and family back home. Check the United States Treasury Department website for the latest guidelines on what specific items and quantities you are allowed to take back with you. Remember, all t-shirts, crafts, knick-knacks, books, etc. technically count as art and can be brought back to the United States without a problem. Just be careful not to take any pre-Revolutionary antiques out of Cuba. They will probably be confiscated at the airport. Keep reading to find out about the art tax you may owe as well on those gifts.

## 75. PACK THE NIGHT BEFORE.

If you plan to go out the night before you return home, pack before heading off to dinner. Cuban concerts and clubs can exude a contagious energy that might make you forget that you have an early morning wake-up call. Don´t get caught off-guard by your alarm clock. Have everything ready to go ahead of time. And, if you want the bellhops to bring your bags down, you have to tell them the day before what time you will be checking out. Give them plenty of buffer time, maybe an hour or so, because no matter how rushed you are, they aren't.

## 76. DOUBLE-CHECK DEPARTURE TIMES FOR YOUR PLANE AND TAXI.

Fortunately, leaving Havana is a breeze compared to the arrival. The airport is less congested, the lines are more organized, and the process is straightforward. Just be sure you are clear on what time your flight is departing. Remember, your cell phone probably won´t automatically remind you of your travel plans or flight schedule changes. Have the hotel call the airport the day before if your flight leaves early in the morning. If you have made prearranged plans for transportation to the airport, be sure all parties are clear on what time and from where you are leaving. If your taxi is late, don´t be shy to bail and take another ride.

# 77. DO A DOCUMENT CHECK.

**P**assport, visa, flight information, and airline ticket....wait, like an actual paper ticket? Yes. Traveling to Cuba is perhaps one of the last places in the world still using the dead tree form of airline tickets. If you were issued a paper ticket, don´t lose it! If you did lose it, go to the airport at least half an hour early and pay (around 10 pesos) to be issued a replacement. If you have lost your visa, you will have to buy a new one at the airport (around 25 pesos). If you lose your passport and don´t realize it until the day of your flight, well, enjoy another day or two in Havana! Check the hotel room safe - reach into all the corners and make sure you got everything before you leave for the airport.

## 78. PAY THE MINIBAR TAB BEFORE BREAKFAST

There is nothing like starting a travel day with an epic line of people trying to check out at the same time. Havana hotels are notorious for being loaded to the brim with group tours thus complicating matters even further. Beat the rush and do your checkout business such as paying the minibar before going to breakfast. Keep your room key and enjoy a few calm minutes while everyone hurries from the dining room to do the check-out routine at the same time. Remember, just because you are in a rush does not mean the hotel desk staff is in a rush.

## 79. EAT A GOOD BREAKFAST AND BRING A SNACK TO THE AIRPORT.

The Jose Marti International Airport is not going to win any travel magazine awards in the next few years. Food options are limited to sandwiches, hot dogs, soft drinks, beer, and coffee. Wait times for flights can be long due to the 4-hour-ahead-of-time check-in, and flight delays of an hour or more are common. Prepare yourself for the long haul and pack a snack (or two) for your travel day.

## 80. HAVE YOUR ART TAX READY.

All pieces of art larger than 200-300 square centimeters need to have an "exportation certificate". This flimsy looking piece of paper is usually included with the sale of most artwork, however, some galleries or street dealers will charge you from 3-10 pesos. Be sure to have it handy just in case you are stopped at the airport and the customs agents ask for proof of payment of art tax. There is also a possibility you will have to pay an extra tax at the airport (less than 10 pesos). Have a few pesos handy just in case. This is not a good time to argue with anyone.

## 81. FIND ONE LAST GOOD PANORAMA.

**W**ith all the checking and gathering up gifts and documents, don't forget to get one last panoramic view of the city before you leave. An early morning walk on the Malecón, a contemplative gaze out of your hotel window, or an early morning coffee in the gardens of the Hotel Nacional overlooking the Atlantic ocean are mental photos that can remind you of why you went to Cuba in the first place.

## 82. JOT DOWN NOTES
## FROM YOUR TRIP.

**B**efore you go home and get flooded with a whole new set of sensory stimuli, jot down notes about your visit. People are going to ask where you went, what you saw, how you felt. Be sure the flood of unchecked emails and messages awaiting you once you reenter the digital world outside of Cuba doesn't push all of those memories out of your head.

## 83. EXCHANGE EMAIL ADDRESSES WITH SOMEONE FROM CUBA.

Contact between Cuba and the outside world has been less than ideal the last half a century. Exchange email addresses with someone you have gotten to know in Cuba Few Cubans have internet in their homes but many have email access through work, a friend, or their cell phone. Use your travel as an opportunity to establish a dialog that can last more than the few days you are on the ground in Havana.

## 84. GIVE UNUSED INTERNET TIME TO A LOCAL.

If connected to the digital world in any way, you probably bought Internet time in the hotel or at an Internet café. If you have any time left, give it to a Cuban. If your hotel has Wi-Fi just look for the young local kids hanging out in the lobby; they are there precisely to use the Internet. Hook them up with more time by giving away your left-over minutes. They will be stoked.

## 85. LEAVE YOUR GUIDEBOOK WITH A CUBAN.

**C**ubans know loads about their country, but there are very few travel books available to them. Maybe you realized when you asked for directions that no one used street names and when you showed a Cuban a map, things just got even more confused. Help improve this situation and leave your guidebook with a local.

## 86. CHECK YOUR DEPARTURE AIRPORT TERMINAL.

The Jose Martì International Airport has two international terminals a few kilometers away from one another. Through early 2015, all direct flights to the United States of America used Terminal 2, with a few other countries thrown in here and there. Terminal 3 is the primary terminal for most international connections. Don´t wind up at the wrong terminal only to have to find another cab once you realize the mistake.

## 87. VISIT DUTY-FREE AT THE AIRPORT.

**N**ow is the time to stock up on a few items to take back to share at home. Duty-Free can be a good place to do last minute shopping in Havana. Rum and coffee come at a discount, as do cigarettes. Cigars are pretty much the same price as in the official cigar outlets in Havana. Buying rum in Duty-Free means you get a better price and you do not have to lug it around Havana with you during your stay. If you have a connecting flight when you get back home, remember to pack those liquids and check your bags. You don't want anyone taking your rum away from you!

## 88. GET A NEWSPAPER.

The news in Cuba comes in two colors: the red ink *Granma* is the "Official Organ of the Communist Party" and the blue ink *Joventud Rebelde* is the youth paper. Aside from the color of the ink, the stories are mostly the same in the each one. These make for interesting conversation pieces back home. Even if you can't read Spanish, you can get the gist of the stories from the expected political context.

## 89. CHANGE YOUR MONEY BACK.

**B**ringing Cuban Pesos home as a souvenir is a good idea, but don´t expect to be able to change them back into local currency. Outside of Cuba the peso is pretty much like Disney Dollars are outside of Disney World: a novelty. Once you have paid any export tax on art and visited the duty-free shops, trade in whatever pesos you are not taking home as gifts or keepsakes.

# WHEN YOU RETURN HOME

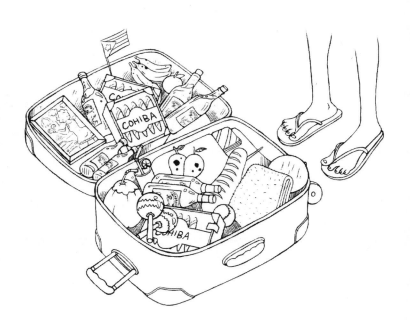

## 90. UNPACK (PHYSICALLY AND MENTALLY).

**H**avana has a tendency to overwhelm the senses, especially if you come from relatively sterile First World suburbia. Many people are overjoyed with the rhythm of Cuban life while others may wonder how in the world Cubans live like they do. Either way, you might have a bit of mental unpacking to take care of before you start gabbing on and on about your experience. Take a quiet moment (or moments) to squeeze all those details out of your short-term memory and be sure they wind up somewhere for safe-keeping. Also, don´t forget to put those cigars you bought in a humidifier.

## 91. MAKE YOUR SOCIAL MEDIA COMEBACK POST.

Once you get back home, with unfettered Internet access, let your friends and family know you have returned. With many changes happening in Cuba and between Cuba and the United States, the island is frequent water cooler talk. Knowing someone who went there recently will interest people more than a trip to Cancun or London. Post a few photos and share a few words about being back home.

## 92. EMAIL SOMEONE IN HAVANA.

While Cubans might not have reliable access to Internet, many have email accounts they can periodically check. Even if you don´t know a word of Spanish, write to the people who gave you their card or exchanged email addresses with you. Cubans love having a connection outside their country as most are well educated about cultures and curious about the world existing beyond the waters surrounding their island. Please note: if you are attaching photos, shrink them down to a smaller size so they can be more easily downloaded.

## 93. GIVE YOUR GIFTS WITH A STORY.

**D**id you buy your cigars on the "informal market"? How hard did you have to bargain for that shawl? Make your gifts more personal than the usual tourist trinkets and try to remember your shopping stories. In Cuba, almost nothing comes easily or without a sideshow. Redeem those moments (which might be frustrating at the time) back home for a few laughs with your friends. The story will stick around long after the 7-year rum is gone.

## 94. DEFINE YOUR EXPERIENCE AS UNIQUE.

Political emotions around Cuba, and opinions of your trip there, can run hot on either side of the ideological spectrum. You will find a few people who have strong opinions that they expect you to share with them. Even if you are the type of person who looks for a good argument, try to present your trip as unique. Remember, you paid for it, you went there, and you made the decisions. The moments that came from that, pleasant or disturbing, are best told with your words and stories. Don´t be afraid to tell it how you experienced it.

## 95. FIND A LOCAL CUBAN CONNECTION.

Almost two million Cubans and their families live outside of Cuba. That means in your hometown, no matter where it is, you are likely to come across someone who once called Havana home. Maybe your short taste of the island left you with a hankering for rice and beans or braised pork loin. Perhaps you want to take up salsa lessons to impress the locals when you make a return trip. You might be surprised to find you can fulfill your Cuban-inspired desires by looking up a local Cuban restaurant or dancing lessons. Cubans are just as curious about what you think of their country as you are about what they think of their homeland.

# 96. STILL CURIOUS? ASK A CUBAN!

A trip to Cuba can usually provoke more questions than answers. There will always be things that surprise you and thoughts that linger after you get home. Plenty of books, articles, and documentaries have been created about Cuba, and those are not bad places to find information. If you want to truly appreciate the diversity of opinions surrounding Cuba, get answers from a Cuban. Maybe it is writing to someone who lives on the island, or talking to your new found local Cuban connection. Trying to wrap your head around a society that is unique in the world is never an easy task; find someone who can do a bit of cultural translating.

## ARROZ CON POLLO (DE DAYNA) – AS INSPIRED BY ABUELA GLORIA JUSTIZ

1/2 a roasted chicken, save meat and discard the bones, skin, fat, etc.
1 cup frozen peas – put to the side with the chicken meat

Sauté ½ cup chopped onions, ½ cup chopped green peppers, and 2 cloves minced garlic in olive oil until soft.

Add:
1 large can diced tomatoes
2 TB lemon juice
2 small or 1 large chicken bouillon cube
2 TB Sazon Completa (Badia brand) seasoning
½ beer
½ cup white wine
salt & pepper to taste
1 cup water
½ package pearl or arborio rice

Cook over medium low heat, stirring often until rice is done. You may have to add more water until rice cooks. When rice is done, stir in the chicken and peas. When chicken and peas are heated through, it is done. Makes two large portions or four small portions.

## 97. HOST A PARTY AND SERVE CUBAN GOODS.

Let's face it - everyone wants cigars and rum from Havana. You will have to decide who gets what. If you have a bunch of friends and not enough to go around, host a party and put everything out for your guests to share. Cook up a big batch of Cuban Arroz con Pollo (chicken and rice). With all those things you stocked up on in Duty-Free, you can make sure everyone gets a taste. Offering gifts and food at a party is doing things *a lo Cubano*.

## 98. SHARE ADVICE BASED ON YOUR EXPERIENCE.

**W**ith tourism to Havana growing rapidly, travelers are always looking for better ways to spend their time, get off the beaten tourist path, and get the best deals. Help your fellow travelers and write emails to people who publish guidebooks if you think you have suggestions on how to do things better or if you followed their advice and it didn´t work out. Check out travel websites and help people make smart travel choices with updated information from your trip. Cuba is a dynamic and changing country - what was relevant may now be out-of-date. Help keep everyone in the know and share your travel experience.

## 99. STAY UP-TO-DATE WITH A CHANGING CUBA.

Sometimes Havana is frustrating, and travelers swear one trip was enough. Others have fantastic experiences and are left with a desire to return. No matter where your opinion falls, try to keep up-to-date about what is going on in Cuba. Maybe your experience wasn't what you expected, or you were completely blown away by your visit. Either way, as long as you keep learning about the place and its people, you might come to understand your visit in a different way. Even though many people associate Havana with a time capsule from the mid-20th century, the island has always been transforming itself and the pace is quickening. One day, many people will realize Havana is no longer what they thought it was. Lots of head scratching will be done, and people will say things like, "I wish I would have gone before…"

# Notes:

*asere*

**Friend.**

## 100. SEND YOUR NEW FRIENDS
## A FEW THINGS THEY MAY NEED.

As the US-Cuban embargo is weakened, much-needed items will begin to trickle into the island at a quicker pace. Right now, if you want to send a small gift to a new friend in Cuba, there are few options. The best (and pretty much only) traditional option from the United States is DHL. The U.S. Postal Service is currently working on better service although it is nowhere near as reliable as DHL at present time. The cheapest and fastest way to get stuff to Havana is to ship it through Miami via a package service specializing in Cuba. You can find dozens of these services with a simple Internet search. Or you can do what Cubans do and look for someone going to the island soon and send it with them.

*Wherever you go, go with all your heart.*

**Confucius**

## 101. START PLANNING YOUR NEXT TRIP.

With the continued loosening of United States regulations surrounding visits to Cuba, don't expect your next visit to the island to be like your last. Cuba is not known for changing quickly, but there is a developing tourist market and foreign investment projects are now being allowed on the island. Keep abreast of these changes as you start planning your next trip. Travel will eventually become easier and cheaper. As more independent travelers explore the country, more Cuban guidebooks will be published. Havana is a great place to start getting to know Cuba. When you return to the island, make a plan to travel in to the provinces to see a very different way of living. Enjoy Cuba for all she offers.

*To meet the people and make new friends.*

**Talk show host Conan O'Brien when asked why he was doing a show from Havana.**

## HAVANA CHECKLIST:

1. Do your homework.
2. Check your passport.
3. Make a budget.
4. Invite a friend.
5. Set realistic expectations.
6. Dust off your dancing shoes.
7. Practice Spanish.
8. Loosen up.
9. Download apps.
10. Invest in travel insurance.
11. Check the weather.
12. Check events calendars.
13. Pack light with space to spare.
14. What clothes to pack.
15. Refill prescriptions and pack over-the-counter meds.
16. Bring hygiene products, sunscreen, and bug spray.
17. Think about gifts.
18. Pack snacks.
19. Buy a humidor.
20. Bring universal electric outlet adaptors.
21. Charge yourself and your batteries.
22. Double and triple-check your reservations.

23. Bring plenty of cash with you.
24. Set your alarm clock.
25. Say *permiso*.
26. Breathe, look, feel.
27. Change and inspect your money.
28. Get small change.
29. Stop trying to check your phone.
30. Reset your internal clock to island time.
31. Don´t be afraid to ask for help.
32. Put on sunscreen and bug repellant.
33. Dress the part.
34. Have a plan but be flexible.
35. Leave gaps in your schedule.
36. Offer to share a cab.
37. Hydrate.
38. Have a laugh!
39. Put on your comfortable shoes.
40. Be an active problem solver.
41. Organize your travel documents.
42. Check in with someone back home.
43. Comfort wins over style.
44. Find shade.
45. Be an impulse buyer.
46. Say *no gracias*.
47. Tip.
48. Step with care.
49. Get up early - at least one day.

50. Try a rum that isn´t Havana Club or a cigar that isn´t Cohiba.
51. Walk on the Malecón.
52. Enjoy the Hotel Nacional patio overlooking the Malecón.
53. Bring an umbrella.
54. Negotiate first and carry exact change.
55. Ride in a convertible.
56. Go to the beach.
57. Gesticulate like you mean it.
58. Ask for directions.
59. Ignore the hustlers.
60. Stay at a casa particular.
61. Eat at only one state-owned restaurant and various paladares.
62. Ask someone what his or her other job is.
63. Send a postcard.
64. Keep your valuables safe.
65. Sit in a park in Vedado.
66. Play or watch a game of dominoes.
67. Tour a cigar factory during reading time.
68. Ferry and walk to giant Jesus.
69. Listen to live music daily.
70. Get off the tourist map.
71. Don't go to the Tropicana.
72. Explore transportation options.
73. Say *gracias*.
74. Pick up gifts for the folks back home.

75. Pack the night before.
76. Double-check departure times for your plane and taxi.
77. Do a document check.
78. Pay the minibar tab before breakfast.
79. Eat a good breakfast and bring a snack to the airport.
80. Have your art tax ready.
81. Find one last good panorama.
82. Jot down notes from your trip.
83. Exchange email addresses with someone from Cuba.
84. Give unused Internet time to a local.
85. Leave your guidebook with a Cuban.
86. Check your departure airport terminal.
87. Visit Duty-Free at the airport.
88. Get a newspaper.
89. Change your money back.
90. Unpack (physically and mentally).
91. Make your social media comeback post.
92. Email someone in Havana.
93. Give your gifts with a story.
94. Define your experience as unique.
95. Find a local Cuban connection.
96. Still curious? Ask a Cuban!
97. Host a party and serve Cuban goods.
98. Share advice based on your experience.
99. Stay up-to-date with a changing Cuba.

100. Send your new friends a few things they may need.
101. Start planning your next trip.

*Visit www.yourdailysuccesstip.com/havana for a printable copy of this list.*

## ABOUT THE AUTHORS

**Dayna Steele**, creator and Chief Tipster for YourDailySuccessTip.com, is known internationally as the *Daily Success Speaker* with her daily tips reaching thousands of success-driven people and companies around the world. A top-rated keynote speaker on effective leadership, productive teamwork, customer service, and employee engagement, Steele inspires and creates success strategies for each audience. She is the creator of the *101 Ways to Rock Your World* book series and the author of the best-selling business book *Rock to the Top: What I Learned about Success from the World's Greatest Rock Stars*. Dayna is also a Rock Radio Hall of Famer and a successful entrepreneur as well as a regular contributor to The Huffington Post. Sign up for her free daily tip at www.YourDailySuccessTip.com.

**Graham Sowa** has lived in Cuba since 2010 as a full-time medical student at the Latin American School of Medicine in Havana. He is completing his last year of studies at the Salvador Allende Hospital in the capital's Cerro neighborhood and dedicates his time not consumed by medicine to helping his fellow Americans make the most out of their visits to Cuba. Graham writes for Havanatimes.org and Oncuba.com as well as reviewing private restaurants in Havana for insightCuba.com. When he graduates from medical school in 2016, he plans to return to Texas to complete his Internal Medicine residency. Graham's short-term goal is to restart the presence of Rotary International in Cuba and promote international professional fellowship. He has given up all hopes of ever learning to dance salsa like a Cuban even though he will be forever tied to the island through his soon-to-be wife Maylin and stepdaughter Gabriela.

**Carlos Paiffer** was born in Havana in 1985. He studied graphic art, digital graphic design, and art education. Still residing in Cuba, he works in audiovisual postproduction, 2D and CGI animation, graphic design, editorial illustrations…and anything else he has been able to teach himself from messing around with fancy editing software and a few how-to videos from YouTube. His most ambitious projects include writing, directing, and producing his own short-film animation and working with known Cuban artists and groups such as Pablo Milanes, Charanga La Habana, and Los Van Van. Carlos is a life long fan of Cuban music and even though his guitar playing and singing are well above par he, like Graham, has abandoned all hope of learning how to dance.

## CONTACT US

**W**e hope you have enjoyed *Havana: 101 Ways to Rock Your World* and are planning your trip! If you have a question, feel free to ask us. And, if you have an idea for another book in the *101 Ways to Rock Your World* book series, let us know. Here is our contact information:

**Dayna Steele**
dayna@yourdailysuccesstip.com

**Graham Sowa**
grahamsowa@gmail.com

**Carlos Iglesias**
carlosmanuel0403@nauta.cu

**Speaking and appearances:**
info@yourdailysuccesstip.com

**Quantity book purchase:**
books@yourdailysuccesstip.com

## FINAL WORDS

I f you had told me this time last year I would be working on a travel guide to Havana, I would have thought you were crazy. A trip to Havana was not going to happen in my lifetime. I figured I would have to rely on the stories, love, food, rum, and cigars from my wonderful in-laws, the Justiz family. But a funny thing happened on the way to 2015…

The following is excerpted from a piece I wrote for *The Huffington Post* in *March 2015:*

*Almost 25 years ago, I had the good fortune of meeting a Cuban-American NASA pilot and marrying into his large, wonderful Cuban-American family. Over the years, we have raised three fine Cuban-American young men who could never quite grasp their heritage. A visit to their dad's roots was not an option until only a few years ago when the U.S. State Department approved educational tours, but the costs associated with such a trip, and family schedules, got in the way time and time again.*

*The planets aligned for Spring Break 2015, and we decided the time was ripe to beat McDonald's and Starbucks to the Justiz family homeland. After much research, a family trip was booked. Less than three weeks later, President Obama announced the easing of Cuban travel restrictions ...*

Here are a few observations and experiences from our weekend in Havana included in The Huffington Post piece:

- *If you want to travel to Cuba, keep in mind things will never work as expected from beginning to end. Memorize the phrase: A lo Cubano.*
- *The check-in process at Miami International takes about four hours. We were about the only people not taking a 50-inch TV back to Cuba. Once on board the charter, three of my children had tickets in row 34 on a plane with only 33 rows. This mom had no "a lo Cubano" for that, and may have frightened a flight attendant or two. Seats were found.*
- *Luggage for all but two people in our tour group of 24 came on another plane, almost three hours*

*later. Those 50-inch TVs apparently took up all the cargo space on our flight.*

- *Cuban customs officials all look like super models, with the women in tight, form-fitting miniskirt uniforms with epaulets and fishnet stockings. You can't make this stuff up.*

- *The first thing you notice when you finally escape the airport is the cars. The cars you have seen in pictures. The cars you wanted to see -- but it turns out to be a very surreal moment standing in the Cuban sun actually next to one. It looked like a movie set to me.*

- *There is a street in Old Havana named for Wonder Husband's paternal grandfather, Tomas Justiz. That is a picture we will cherish.* (Send us a picture of you in front of this street sign and we will send you a prize. Not sure what, but we will come up with something!)

- *We met cousins who were born after the revolution. Our dinner invitation was met with tears. Food is still rationed to the locals in Cuba.*

- *The cost for a trip to Cuba from the U.S., done properly and legally, ran us about $3,000 per person minimum for four days including air, hotel, transportation, fees, visas, guide, etc. There are still forms upon forms to fill out and going with an established tour company made the whole process much easier.*

- *As soon as you arrive at the Havana airport, you see the lack of efficiency or even space for all the passengers arriving. There aren't enough bathrooms, and there is no food or water until you pass through customs -- which for us was a several hour process. Flights and hotels are at a premium right now; the infrastructure is just not there for the sheer number of people who want to visit Cuba. It probably will be -- along with McDonald's and Starbuck's -- in a few years. You need that patience thing again.*

*I could write for days and never be able to sum up the sights, sounds, feelings, confusion, elation, and politics of Cuba. What I can say is this: Cuba was the flavor of the Caribbean, the iron balconies and street music of New Orleans, the political suppression and fear of Russia, the poverty of Mexico, the quaint sidewalk cafes of Europe, the corner parks of New York City, and the family love of Miami.*

Thanks to my first guide through Havana and the co-author of this book, Graham Sowa. I can't wait to go back and visit the Sowa family in Cuba. To illustrator Carlos, who I can't wait to actually meet in person someday in Havana. And, to InsightCuba's Tom Popper for the Introduction he wrote for this book and for the work his company does. It changed my life for the better.

Thanks to longtime *Steeleworker* Charlene Hall for her editing help – much appreciated. To friend and *In the Classroom* co-author Linda Lee who always finds time to do an edit pass through all my books and then join me for wine. And, to my brother-in-law Ralph Gazitua for the multiple introductions he has made and help he has given with this book.

I never thought Wonder Husband and I would see Cuba together, always thinking it was something my kids would do in the future. The fact we did it as a family, including our new bonus daughter, was a life-changing experience for each of us.

You'll see the word *check* a lot in this book - check your flights, double-check your documents, triple-check you have your passport, etc. Things are changing in Cuba and with change come confusion and resistance. The correct way of doing things changes daily. Take a big yoga breath and go with the flow. This is going to be a wild ride.

Thinking of Cuba takes my breath away – literally. I hold my breath waiting to see what will happen with the changes, the people, the government, with everything. I can't wait to go back. At the same time, I am frightened I'll never go back, that something will happen to wake me up from this dream.

And finally from that Huffington Post piece:

*I have been tied to Cuba by marriage for almost 25 years. I am now tied to Cuba by hope.*

Dayna Steele
Creator, *101 Ways to Rock Your World*
CEO *YourDailySuccessTip.com*

**Notes:**

**Notes:**

*Salud, dinero, y amor - y tiempo para disfrutarlos.*

**Gloria Justiz family toast: Health, money and love - and the time to enjoy them.**

**Daily Success**

THE BOOK SERIES

Made in the USA
Middletown, DE
24 August 2015